Contents

Ducks

Ducks are birds
with strong bills
and webbed feet.
Young ducks are
called ducklings.

Ducks and their ducklings
live near lakes and ponds.

A female is a duck.

Sometimes a female

is called a hen.

A male is a drake.

Drakes and ducks mate.

hen

drake

Laying eggs

Most ducks lay 4 to 12 eggs.

A duck sits on her eggs

to keep them warm.

Ducklings

Ducklings hatch after about one month. A duckling breaks the egg open with its egg tooth.

egg tooth

Ducklings have soft feathers called down. Ducklings will grow new feathers after two months.

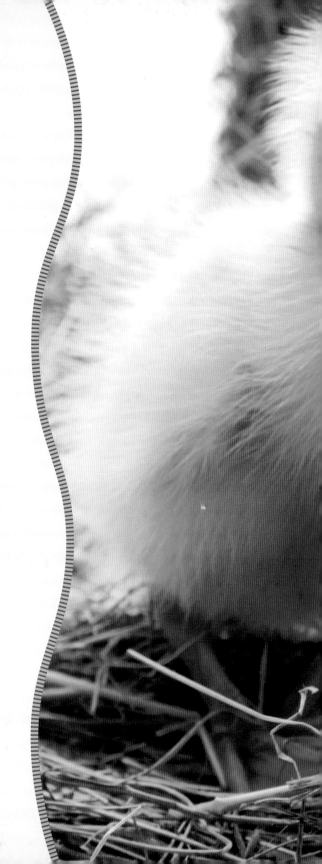

Growing up

Ducklings follow their mother
to the water. She teaches
them to swim and to dive.

Ducklings become adults.

Drakes and ducks fly.

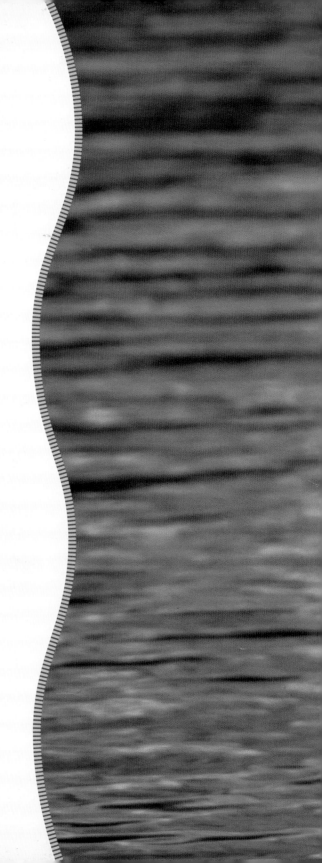

Watch ducks grow

hatching

adult after about
four to five months

Glossary

bill hard part of a bird's mouth; ducks use
their bills to peck at food; bills are also called beaks

bird warm-blooded animal with wings, two legs and
feathers; birds lay eggs; most birds can fly

egg tooth tooth-like part that sticks out on a duckling's bill;
the egg tooth falls off shortly after the duckling hatches

feather one of the light, fluffy parts that covers the skin on
a bird's body; ducks have waterproof feathers

hatch break out of an egg; ducklings hatch from
their eggs after about one month

mate join together to produce young

webbed having folded skin or tissue between
an animal's toes or fingers; ducks have webbed feet
to help them swim better

Find out more

Books

Ducklings (Explore My World), Marfe Ferguson Delano (National Geographic Kids, 2017)

Ducks (Farm Animals), Michelle Hasselius (Raintree, 2017)

Farm Animals (Tadpoles Learners), Annabelle Lynch (Franklin Watts, 2015)

Websites

www.activityvillage.co.uk/ducks
Activity Village

www.bbc.co.uk/cbeebies/watch/andys-baby-animals-ducklings
BBC

Comprehension questions

1. What things do ducklings learn from their mother?

2. Ducks are described as having webbed feet. What does "webbed" mean?

3. How do ducklings hatch?

Index